Reading
The Diary of
Anne Frank

THE ENGAGED
READER

Reading
The Diary of
Anne Frank

Neil Heims

CHELSEA HOUSE PUBLISHERS

VP, NEW PRODUCT DEVELOPMENT Sally Cheney
DIRECTOR OF PRODUCTION Kim Shinners
CREATIVE MANAGER Takeshi Takahashi
MANUFACTURING MANAGER Diann Grasse

Staff for READING THE DIARY OF ANNE FRANK

EDITOR Matt Uhler
PHOTO EDITOR Sarah Bloom
PRODUCTION EDITOR Bonnie Cohen
EDITORIAL ASSISTANT Sarah Sharpless
SERIES DESIGNER Takeshi Takahashi
COVER DESIGNER Takeshi Takahashi
LAYOUT EJB Publishing Services

www.chelseahouse.com

First Printing

9 8 7 6 5 4 3 2 1

Library of Congress Cataloging-in-Publication Data

Heims, Neil.
  Reading the diary of Anne Frank / Neil Heims.
      p. cm. — (The engaged reader)
  Includes bibliographical references.
  ISBN 0-7910-8829-4
  1. Frank, Anne, 1929-1945—Diaries—Juvenile literature. 2. Holocaust,
Jewish (1939-1945)—Netherlands—Amsterdam—Personal narratives—
Juvenile literature. 3. Amsterdam (Netherlands)—Ethnic relations—Juvenile
literature. 4. Jews—Netherlands—Amsterdam—Diaries—Juvenile litera-
ture. I. Title. II. Series.
  DS135.N6F733436 2005
  940.53'18'092—dc22
                                                  2005009523

Table of Contents

Assumptions and Context: Before You Read Anne Frank's *Diary*

A DIARY THAT LOOKS LIKE A NOVEL

IF SOMEONE HANDED YOU a copy of *The Diary of Anne Frank*[1] without telling you anything about it, one of the first questions you might ask as you began reading it is, what kind of book is this? Is it really a diary or is it a novel pretending to be a diary? Many novels, after all, have been written in the form of a series of letters to an imaginary friend, as is *The Diary of Anne Frank*.

You would quickly realize that if this is a novel in letter form, it is a historical novel. All the events of the book take place against the background of the Nazi German invasion of Holland during World War Two, and each letter is dated. The dates themselves suggest the terrible reality, besides the war, which haunted the world in the years 1942, 1943, and 1944: all the Jews of Europe were being rounded up by the Nazis in order to be exterminated. And you would quickly realize, as you continued to read, that the narrator-heroine of the book is a Jewish girl—13 years old when she started keeping a diary, 15 when she was forced to stop—whose family and some of their acquaintances are in hiding from the Nazis. Surprisingly, too, you would realize that despite the overwhelming historical pressure on Anne and the people she writes about, the diary is very much a domestic story and the story of a girl's rite of passage from girlhood to young womanhood. It is full of the typical problems you would expect a girl to experience even in an ordinary time.

Would it matter to you as a reader if the book were not a novel but an actual diary, if the story you are reading were not "made up" but was an actual account of what was happening? Would it make a difference as far as the experience of reading is concerned? Clearly it would. What kind of difference? Why?

If Anne Frank's *Diary* were a work of imaginative fiction, a novel and not a diary, it would not necessarily, be any less "true." A work of fiction is not a lie. Fiction reassembles and reconstructs reality in order to convey truth. We look for truth in stories all the time. So, if Anne Frank was a fictional character invented by a writer, and if that fictional character was presented through the diary she is presumably writing, we could still be deeply moved by her story and her character. We would still have a penetrating description of people adapting to extraordinary circumstances. We would be right in saying that the novel, even though fiction, could still strongly present important aspects of how people lived and behaved under Nazi rule.

Anne Frank's *Diary*, however, is not a work of fiction; it is not a novel. It is a historical document that describes for succeeding generations what life was like as the Nazis sought to make life unlivable for Jews. But it is also more than a historical document of an atrocity: it is a work of literature. As such, it is a document of the human spirit as people attempted to survive when their very humanity was being threatened by organized inhumanity. Anne Frank was so close, yet so calm, a fluent observer of events, of her own consciousness, of other people's behavior, and of the world surrounding her. She brought her experiences to life, and as a result her diary reads like a novel.

Despite the excruciating circumstances she wrote about, she was never overwrought. Anne was always in control of her material; overwhelming though her brief life was, she was never overwhelmed by it, but was even able to narrate her panic, fear, and distress with a novelist's combination of immediacy and detachment.

The fact that Anne Frank's *Diary* is a diary and not a work of fiction gives it the kind of sanctity and power that monuments and tombstones can sometimes possess. Reading it, we are in the presence of something real. With a sense of awe, we comprehend that a girl so young faced a frightfully brutal situation with steadiness and wrote about it with such clarity, insight, and meticulous calm that, in the midst of it, she was able to grow in wisdom and humanity. Anne Frank's *act* of writing, not only *what* she wrote, is conveyed in the diary. Consequently, the diary imparts a sense of faith in the possibility of humanity for both the writer and reader, rather than despair at the brutality and negation characteristic of such inhumanity.

Readers of Anne Frank's *Diary* are in an unusual relation to the author. Unlike the common situation when we read a story—the author knows more than the reader and artfully reveals information for maximum dramatic effect—when we read Anne Frank's *Diary*, we know more than she does about the story she is writing if we know about that piece of history. We are not in suspense about the big issue. We know that the people in hiding will, in all likelihood, be found and that there is grim death lurking in the concentration camps that they are sent to. We know that Anne will not escape. While the possibility of this terrible end haunts her, Anne continues, nevertheless, moment to moment, day by day, to live and to write, and to believe in the alternative possibility: that the war will end, that fascism (the extreme nationalism of the Nazis) will be defeated, and that she will come out of hiding to live a full, rich, and useful life. The act of faith in life that Anne shows by writing is vindicated by us as readers. Although we know what she does not know, either as character or as author (that she will not survive), we also know that her book will survive and keep her and every other victim of Nazi brutality a vital part of our individual and collective memories. That is the most important part of the story. Through the composition of this diary, Anne Frank vanquished those who sought to conquer her. In a way, she defeated death by living on through her diary.

The Diary of Anne Frank, then, is a diary, a document, and a testament, but it reads like a novel. There is an ongoing story with a cast of characters. The book recounts their actions, probes their personalities, and provides moments of suspense and revelation. The setting is vividly drawn, and a reader can detect themes emerging from the events Anne recounts. Moreover, even though it is an unfinished work, structurally, the diary offers its readers a complete experience. It has a beginning, middle, and end, as does the story of its composition and eventual publication. For that story, however, we must look at the social and political context—the rise of Nazism—and at the human context—the life of the Frank family before they went into hiding.

THE HISTORICAL CONTEXT: NAZISM

In 1933, Adolf Hitler was elected chancellor of Germany. As chancellor he ushered in an era as brutal, dreadful, and murderous as any in recorded history. Hitler's rise to power was a victory for the fascist Nazi Party. The cornerstone of Nazi belief was the idea of race: that there were superior and inferior people and that the difference between people was inescapably determined by racial identity.

Under Nazi rule, Germans were seen to be members of a "master race," and Jews were defined as being members of an inferior race—not really human beings but vermin, as they were characterized in a Nazi propaganda film of 1940, Fritz Hippler's *Die Ewige Jude* (*The Eternal Jew*). By visually alternating images of rats and Jews, the film portrayed Jews as dangerous to the health, wealth, and moral integrity of the German people. The necessity for their extermination, the film asserted, was as self-evident as the need to exterminate rats and should cause no greater distress. The Nazis under Hitler were to carry this idea to its ultimate, horrific conclusion.

After Hitler came to power in 1933, a series of laws were passed making life for Jewish people extremely difficult and ultimately impossible to maintain. Systematically, Jews were prevented from practicing their professions, holding jobs in universities, hospitals, law firms, or publishing houses. They had to give up their businesses. Jews were forced to live in all-Jewish neighborhoods and their children were forced to go to all-Jewish schools. The Nuremberg Laws of 1935 made marriage between Jews and non-Jews illegal, and Jews were forced to wear a yellow identification badge in the shape of the six-pointed Star of David at all times. Much worse was to follow, particularly the round-up of all Jews and their deportation to concentration camps equipped with gas chambers and crematoria, where millions were tortured, brutalized, and murdered.

Nazi ambition was not limited to Germany, nor was their will to dominate and exterminate limited to the persecution of Jews. They also sought to eliminate Gypsies, homosexuals, communists, and the weak. In 1937, with the invasion of Czechoslovakia, the Third Reich—as Germany under Hitler was called—began a campaign for world conquest and subordination to German power. Two years later, when Germany invaded Poland, World War Two began in Europe.

ON YOUR OWN
ACTIVITY #1

The events we read about in Anne Frank's *Diary* took place toward the end of the Nazi period, which began with the rise to power of Adolf Hitler and the Nazi Party in 1933 and ended in 1945 with the Allied forces defeat of Germany in the Second World War. There were a series of events—acts of legislation against Jews, anti-Jewish street riots, anti-Jewish propaganda—which preceded the actual program of extermination the Nazis carried out against European Jews in the 1940s. Using the Internet and/or the library, construct a chronological table tracing the course of the Nazi campaign against Jews.

THE FRANKS

Anne's father, Otto Frank, realized the dangers posed by Nazism early on, and in 1933, he moved his family from Frankfurt, Germany, to Amsterdam, Holland. Otto had been born in Frankfurt in 1889 to a well-to-do family. His father owned and directed a bank, Banksgeschaft Michael Frank. Otto graduated from the Lessing Gymnasium (a gymnasium is a high school) in 1908 and enrolled in the University of Heidelberg. He left Heidelberg after one semester to go to New York City with Nathan Strauss, a classmate at Heidelberg and a member of the family that owned Macy's department store.

Otto worked in Macy's for a year, returned to Germany in 1909 following his father's death, and continued to study business administration in Dusseldorf. In 1915, Otto joined the German army, fought in the artillery on the Western Front in World War One, and was a lieutenant by the end of the war. As a civilian, Otto resumed his position in the family bank, but business was terrible. During the 1920s, Germany experienced a galloping inflation that made German currency nearly valueless. Otto visited Amsterdam during these years in order to establish a business there, but that business failed. In 1925, Otto married Edith Hollander, the daughter of a manufacturer in Aachen, Germany. They had two children: Margot, born in 1926, and Anne, born on June 12, 1929.

The Franks lived quietly in Holland during the 1930s. Anne was a happy child with a lively disposition and a spunky, self-assertive nature, capable of winning over teachers who became exasperated with her. Anne's entry for June 21, 1942, written less than a month before she went into hiding, exemplifies this capability. In that entry Anne tells of how Mr. Keptor, the math teacher became annoyed with her ceaseless talking and assigned to her a composition on the subject, "A Chatterbox." Anne wrote the subject down in her notebook and tried to keep quiet. When she finished her homework later that night, Anne saw the title of her composition written in her notebook and began to ponder the subject. She reasoned, "…anyone can scribble some nonsense in large letters with the words well spaced but the difficulty was to prove beyond doubt the necessity of talking." Anne formulated an idea and wrote her paper. In her composition she argued that talking was a feminine characteristic of which she "should never be cured." She also argued that her mother talked a lot and suggested that she could do little about inherited qualities. Her teacher, laughing at her arguments, might have been willing to forgive Anne, but when she continued to talk, he gave her another composition, "Incurable Chatterbox." She again wrote out her composition to the satisfaction of Mr. Keptor, and was without punishment for two days. When once again her talking became too much for her teacher, Mr. Keptor announced to the class "Anne, as punishment for talking, will do a composition entitled 'Quack, quack, quack, says Mrs. Natterbeak.'" Though the assignment was intended to make a fool of Anne, she figured she could get her revenge by writing the entire assignment as a poem. Her poem told the story of a mother duck, a father swan, and their three baby ducklings. In the story, the baby ducklings are bitten to death by the father because they "chattered too much." Her teacher saw the joke and read the poem aloud to several of his classes. Anne concludes this episode by saying, "Since then I am allowed to talk, never get extra work, in fact Keptor always jokes about it."[2]

In nearly every one of the many pictures of her that remain, Anne shows a natural and unforced smile. Her account of her birthday celebration, in a diary entry dated June 15, 1942, provides a good description of what her life in Amsterdam was like before she was forced into hiding. In that entry she talks of passing cookies out to her teachers and classmates, and how she was allowed to choose which game they would play at gym—as it was her birthday. She also talks of how her friends came home with her that day, and reflects on her friends Hanneli and Sanne, "People who saw us together used to say, 'There goes Anne, Hanne and Sanne.'"[3]

In Amsterdam, Otto Frank established a business, Opekta, to manufacture fruit products, especially pectin for making jam; and spices used in processing sausages, and he was one of its managing directors. The sausage spice end of the business was run by Mr. van Pels—Anne called him "van Daan" in her diary—who went into hiding with the Franks along with his wife and teenage son, Peter. The Opekta office, factory, and warehouse were all located in a tall, rather narrow building at 263 Prinsengracht in Amsterdam. The building still stands and is the site of the Anne Frank Museum. In the rear attic of this building, which Anne called the "Secret Annex," the Franks, the van Pels, and a dentist named Pfeffer, whom Anne called "Dussel," hid from the Nazis.

In 1940, the Nazis invaded Holland. As they did in each country they conquered, they established full control of all the institutions and ran them according to German policies. Soon, Jews were cut out of Dutch society (denied the rights and protections guaranteed to the citizens of Holland), forced out of businesses, segregated among themselves, and ultimately shipped off to Germany or Eastern Europe to be slave laborers or to be killed in the Nazi death camps.

Under the Nazi decrees, Otto was officially disconnected from his business, Anne and Margot were forced to attend an all-Jewish school, and the whole family's movements were restricted to the point that they were forbidden to use the buses and compelled to turn in their bicycles. That was only the beginning of the Nazi program, which was to culminate in deportation and death. When Margot received an order to report for deportation to a slave labor camp, the Frank family went into hiding in the Opekta building. They moved into the Secret Annex.

THE HELPERS

The strategy of going into hiding in the middle of a major Nazi-occupied European city required a great deal of planning, coordination, and several trustworthy allies. A group of people risked their own lives to protect Anne and her family and friends. They appear repeatedly in Anne's diary,

ON YOUR OWN
ACTIVITY #2

Part of Adolf Hitler's grand design was the conquest of Europe and the establishment of an empire to be called Germania, of which Berlin would be the capital. In order to reach that goal, the Nazis invaded and occupied nearly every European country. In some countries, Nazi occupation was generally accepted by the people (always excluding the Jews, who were sent to labor and death camps), and in some countries, undergrounds (secret groups) were formed and occupation was resisted. Often both responses occurred. Using the Internet and/or the library, discuss the response of the people in six European countries of your choosing to the Nazi invasion, occupation, and general treatment of the Jews.

bringing food, gifts, and news of the outside world. These protectors, most of them colleagues of Otto's at Opekta, first helped him prepare the hiding space by transporting necessities there for a year before they went into hiding. They also helped spread the cover story that the Franks had managed to get through Nazi lines and escape to Belgium, so that after they disappeared they would not be looked for in Amsterdam. Among the protectors, the one who stands out most for the reader is Miep Gies.

THE DIARY

Anne Frank's diary was found by Miep, strewn on the floor in the attic of the Secret Annex, after its inhabitants had been taken by the Nazi Green Police in a raid on August 4, 1944. The diary was written in two books and on loose sheets of paper. The first diary was written in an actual diary with a red plaid binding that Anne was given for her thirteenth birthday. Anne's first entry is her account of her first encounter with the diary itself: "Soon after seven I went to Mummy and Daddy and then to the sitting room to undo my presents. The first to greet me was *you*, possibly the nicest of all."[4]

The second diary was written in an office notebook that Miep gave Anne after she had used up the pages in her plaid diary. Miep kept both volumes and the loose sheets of paper until after the war. When Anne's father returned to Amsterdam—the only one of the eight hiding in the Secret Annex not to perish in the concentration camps—Miep gave him all of Anne's writing, the diaries and several stories Anne had been working on. "I just picked it up in order to give it to Anne when she would return," Miep said later.[5]

Otto Frank lightly edited his daughter's diary, removing

material that cast Anne's mother in a negative light and passages in which Anne discussed sexuality, anatomy, and adolescent development. In *The Diary of Anne Frank*: the 1991 edition, called *The Definitive Edition*, these passages were restored to the text. That edition was prepared from the several texts brought together in The Critical Edition of *The Diary of Anne Frank*, published in 1986. The Critical Edition reproduces Anne's complete original diary, the revisions she began after she thought she might be able to publish her diary as a novel after the war, and the diary as it was originally edited and published by Otto Frank.

Narrative Technique

THE NARRATOR AS WITNESS

ON THE INSIDE COVER of Anne Frank's *Diary*, before the first page, she pasted a picture of herself seated at a desk before an open book of blank pages. The first words she wrote in her diary are "Gorgeous photograph isn't it!!!!"[6]

Spunky self-mockery and self-revelation are combined in Anne's comic expression. Anne's diary is a kind of narrative photograph, a picture in words, intended to convey her personality, what her life is like, and who she is. She writes as if speaking to the diary itself:

> I hope I will be able to confide everything to you, as I have never been able to confide in anyone, and I hope you will be a great source of comfort and support.[7]

A diarist is like the first-person narrator of a novel. Everything is seen from Anne's point of view—she is the "I" of the story. In a novel, first-person narration is a technique, a storytelling strategy. It influences the way we digest the information of the novel and it warns us that what we are reading constitutes only one particular point of view. A narrator-centered point of view does not detract from the quality of a novel. In fact, it may add to its complexity; it can signal to the reader that the story being told is a subjective or personal account, not necessarily representing the way things are in reality but rather the way one person sees them.

In a first-person, narrator-centered novel, nevertheless, there is still a controlling author who is different from the narrator. The author decides, for the sake of the story, what the narrator will know and will not know, and when. This, of course, also determines how the story unfolds for the reader. In the case of an actual diary, the author of the diary is identical to its narrator and has no knowledge beyond the narrator's. The reader, because of historical circumstances, may, in fact, actually know more than the author about the events described.

In a diary, a first-person account is inevitable, rather than being a narrative strategy: a diary is the record of a voice talking as itself, to itself. Since Anne Frank is a diarist not a novelist (although she writes about other people as well as about herself), the result is that her descriptions of others really serves to reveal something about herself. Other characters are included in the diary because of their relation to Anne. Although they influence her and she affects them, the diary is about her. Even while writing about them, Anne is telling the story of herself, and, by doing that, by confiding to her diary, she creates a sense of self not only for those who read the diary but for herself.

The imaginative act that allowed her narrative self-creation is that she transformed the diary into an actual person to whom she eagerly communicated her experiences, thoughts, and feelings and through whom she could make herself known. Her diary became an imaginary friend she called "Kitty."[8]

It is not, however, only the invention of "Kitty" that kept the diary from being a series of "bald facts" or disconnected events, reveries, or adventures. Once her family was in hiding, the diary acquired a unifying theme and narrative direction: what is it like to be in hiding?

ON YOUR OWN
ACTIVITY #3

Anne Frank's *Diary* is written, since it is a diary, in the first person by a narrator who does not know what will happen next. But we who live more than half a century after the events she chronicles do. Select a portion of the diary you find particularly interesting, moving, or significant and, using the setting, the characters, the events, and the themes presented in the diary, make that section the basis for a short story narrated by an omniscient (all-knowing) third-person narrator.

Will the people in hiding survive or perish? Unlike the author of a novel, Anne did not know or control the outcome of the story. Unlike the reader of a novel, the reader of Anne's diary presumably begins knowing its author's fate, for that lies outside the narrative boundaries of the diary.

Because of the reader's historical knowledge of things that Anne did not know, which will affect her, her characters, and the story she tells, the reader becomes a co-narrator, someone whose knowledge adds to Anne's narrative. The reader's knowledge, the historical story the reader brings to the diary, gives added depth, breadth, and emotional power to Anne's story, tragically filling it out. This is especially so because Anne's diary is not a series of frightened or depressed complaints but a detailed, engaging account of life as it was experienced in an ongoing present. The very ordinariness of life and of the people in the Secret Annex makes the story in the diary extraordinary.

Anne's narrative technique is simple and direct. Throughout the diary, she says beforehand what she intends to do as narrator, and then she does it. At the moment of transition from making diary entries to writing letters to Kitty, for example, Anne lays out her writing strategy. In her entry for Saturday, 20 June, 1942, she states, "I will start by sketching in brief the story of my life," and in the very next paragraph begins to do so.[9]

She continues, discussing how "the rest of our family ... felt the full impact of Hitler's anti-Jewish laws," how some escaped to the United States, and then how the Germans invaded Holland and began persecuting Jews there. "So far," Anne concludes, "everything is all right with the four of us and here I come to the present day."[10]

Having brought the imaginary reader up to date, Anne begins the entry for June 20, 1942, anew, this time addressing it "Dear Kitty" saying, "I'll start right away." This artless directness marks Anne's writing throughout the diary: "I'll begin from the moment I got you, the moment I saw you lying on the table among my other birthday presents." Similar instances of Anne's directness can be found throughout her diary in such entries as the ones found for Wednesday, 24 June, 1942; Tuesday, 30 June, 1942; Monday, 21 September, 1942; Friday, 23 July, 1943, and so on. These are only a few instances of Anne's way of announcing a theme or an event. As introductions or transitions, such sentences may reveal a certain lack of sophistication—they seem like the author's notes to herself—but they are also charged with an immediacy that is perfectly suited to the circumstances and the subject. They show how Anne combines plan and execution, making the diary the story of its composition as well as a chronicle of events.

Anne's comfortable, talkative style, moreover, is not flat. After she says what she is going to do, she tells her story, and the story itself needs nothing more than the detailed simplicity of her direct account to be exciting:

> Margot and I began to pack some of our most vital belongings into a school satchel. The first thing I put in was this diary, then hair curlers, handkerchiefs, schoolbooks, a comb, old letters; I put in the craziest things with the idea that we were going into hiding. But I'm not sorry, memories mean more to me than dresses.
>
> At five o'clock Daddy finally arrived ...[11]

That everything is seen and narrated from Anne's point

of view does not limit or narrow the scope of the diary. Anne's being at the center of the story, however, defines the diary as a story of Anne's consciousness. Writing is her way of asserting consciousness, when it is threatened, of being alive and aware in the midst of forces that have been mobilized to deny life to her. Despite the view of Jews spread by the Nazis, Anne's diary shows, because of the very project of recording her life, that such a life—the life of an ordinary Jewish girl—is not worthless but glows with humanity. It is full of the meaning, thought, opinion, and feeling that she discovers through telling stories about her experiences and the people who share them. As long as she is writing, Anne is in control of the narrative of her life, not the Nazi persecutors, because as a writer she defines what it is to be human.

Along with the direct simplicity of Anne's narrative style is its economy. She captures a scene, conveys action, presents her characters effortlessly, it seems, and without wasting words. Her 1944 entry describing a break-in at the warehouse does just that.

> Peter was on the landing when he heard two loud bangs. He went downstairs and saw that a large panel was missing from the left half of the warehouse door. He dashed upstairs, alerted the "Home Guard," and the four of them went downstairs. When they entered the warehouse, the burglars were going about their business. Without thinking, Mr. van Daan yelled "Police!" Hurried footsteps outside; the burglars had fled. The board was put back in the door so the police wouldn't notice the gap, but then a swift kick from outside sent it flying to the floor.[12]

In the very midst of a situation fraught with anxiety and

terror, Anne writes with a quiet steadiness. She renders complex actions with an artless clarity.

NARRATIVE ELEMENTS: DESCRIPTION, DIALOGUE, REFLECTION

Anne's strength as a diarist is that her narrative is not a monologue. By bringing to her diary the techniques of a novelist, she succeeded in creating a picture of her world and her place in it. She accumulated bits and pieces of life in hiding, and she strung them together by her direct and conversational tone. The separate elements are unified simply because they happened to her and she reported them. Examine the entry for Saturday, 27 February, 1943. In this entry she considers Churchill's pneumonia; a copy of the Bishop's letter to churchgoers; the sale of the house; a card index in which she and Margot can write down the books they have read; the states of her families various relationships; and the rationing of butter and margarine.[13]

These are accounts of random events that are not even brought together by connecting sentences. Each paragraph is independent of the others, and their order does not reflect a continuous narrative. However, that does not really matter because the paragraphs contribute to a complete picture of life in the Secret Annex. One paragraph, reporting events outside Anne's immediate environment, concerns the Dutch bishops' call for resistance to the Nazis. Another concerns the immediate "adventure" of living in hiding: the building has been sold, and there is a risk that the new owner will discover the Jews hidden in the Secret Annex if he inspects the building. Yet another paragraph is a tidbit about how Anne is going to keep track of the books she reads and write down new vocabulary words. This is a detail that might fit into any schoolgirl's diary—so is the mother/daughter tension she alludes to in the paragraph following. The last paragraph concerns food rationing and how it affects the group living together in hiding. What unifies this mix of ordinary and exceptional matter is that collectively these paragraphs present Anne's life in all its aspects: a picture of the common, everyday events of a life that is not ordinary because of persecution. Because ordinary events of life still occur under extraordinary circumstances, they take on enormous interest.

In the following extract, Anne starts characteristically with an artless announcement, "The title for this piece is: 'The communal task of the day: potato peeling!'" There follows a bare-bones description of the scene, including each person's contribution to the job: "One person fetches the newspapers, another the knives (keeping the best for himself, of course), a third potatoes and the fourth a pan of water." Then, once she has the people assembled, Anne begins describing each person by describing his or her approach to the job of potato peeling and by detailing their interactions, first focusing on herself and Mr. Dusssel:

> Mr. Dussel begins, does not always scrape well, but scrapes incessantly, glancing right and left. Does everyone do it the way he does?

Anne shifts attention to her father, and even her description of the way he peels potatoes reveals the depth of her feeling for him:

I scrape on again. Now I look to the other side, where Daddy is sitting; for him scraping potatoes is not just a little odd job, but a piece of precision work.

Then Anne turns to Mrs. van Daan, briefly describing her failed flirtatiousness with Dussel, but quickly moving to a dialogue between her and her husband. In that short exchange, Anne captured what is probably the essence of their married life.

Here is a group of people living under very difficult and dangerous circumstances, their humanity and their lives hanging by a thread, and the task at hand for them, the thing they must do, is peel potatoes. As narrator, Anne does not draw attention to the profound irony or incongruity in this situation, although a reader will. That is what makes the common tedium and bickering arising from a circle of potato peelers worth reading about. Not only can evil, as the philosopher Hannah Arendt argued in her book *Eichman in Jerusalem,* be banal or commonplace, but the act of evading it can also be banal. Courage

ON YOUR OWN
ACTIVITY #4

Begin to keep a diary of your own. You might want to look in a stationery store for a notebook and a pen you particularly like. If you are into computers, you might prefer to begin blogging—keeping an online journal. Be aware, though, that although a diary can be private and you may choose to show it only to people you want to see it or to keep it entirely secret, a web blog is a very public thing. How might this difference between keeping a diary and blogging affect what you write and how you write?

is not always as dramatic as it is often depicted to be in the movies.

Without any narrative intervention and without calling the reader's attention to it, Anne has presented some psychological effects of waiting in hiding. Mrs. van Daan finds an outlet for the frustration of being confined by needling her husband. Mr. van Daan suppresses the doubts his wife expresses in order to keep himself from falling into despair. He inevitably snaps at her when she continually taunts him with his own unexpressed fears. Anne does not draw these conclusions herself. They are the result of the co-narration added by the reader.

The most significant psychological relationship in the diary, of course, is Anne's relationship with herself, the way she observes and thinks about her own experiences and reflects upon her own growth. She writes about her reflections with the same clarity, directness, and honesty with which she writes about everything else. In a comment she added in January 1944, Anne wrote with psychological keenness about longing for her cat, Mootje: "The whole time I've been here I've longed unconsciously—and at times consciously—for trust, love and physical affection. This longing may change in intensity, but it is always there."[14]

Or consider the complexity she brought to a reflection about her relationship with Peter van Daan the day after their first passionate kisses:

> Peter's reached a part of me that no one has ever reached before, except in my dream! He's taken hold of me and turned me inside out. Doesn't everyone need a little quiet time to put

themselves to rights again? Oh, Peter, what have you done to me? What do you want from me?[15]

IRONY: AN UNINTENDED NARRATIVE ELEMENT

When Anne wrote, "There's a time and a place for both, but how can I be sure that I've chosen the right time?", it was a serious, straightforward question for her, one that can haunt any of us at times in our lives. But the circumstances in which Anne was living when she asked that question tinged it with irony.

Irony is a narrative tool writers often employ to show how the unknown can intersect with what a character thinks she knows. The effect is to give breadth and dimension to a story, warning us that things are not always what they seem—and not to be too sure of what you think you are

ON YOUR OWN
ACTIVITY #5

Personification is defined as a figure of speech in which an inanimate object takes on human qualities, or are represented in human form. Given this definition of personification, do you think Anne's treatment of her diary, "Kitty," qualifies as an example of personification? Would it have been more or less effective if Anne had assigned to her diary qualities other than the ability to "listen?" How might the narrative have been different if the diary spoke back to Anne? Finally, consider the importance personification plays in helping Anne create an "audience" for her writing, and the unintended irony that her writing found a real audience. On your own, try picking an ordinary object and begin writing to it or about it as though it were a person.

sure of. Irony marks the discrepancy between what the author knows and chooses to share with the reader and what the character in the story knows—what, that is, the author chooses to withhold from the character. Since the separation between author and character does not exist for the diarist, narrative irony is a function only of a reader's awareness. It is an unintended narrative element. In Anne Frank's *Diary*, the very fact of its unintendedness gives the irony a peculiar poignancy. It does not matter for Anne whether or not it is the right time because, for her, it is the only time. We know—but she can only hope and act as if it is not so—that the time she is living in is, for her, the end of time.

■ Anne Frank was 13 years old when her family went into hiding from the Nazis in 1942. The diary she kept, first published in 1947, is a cherished testament to the human spirit.

■ Anne was a happy child with a lively disposition and a self-assertive nature. This photo was taken on her tenth birthday in 1939. Anne is second from the left.

■ Anne Frank's *Diary* was written in two books and on loose sheets. The first book was this plaid journal given to Anne on her thirteenth birthday.

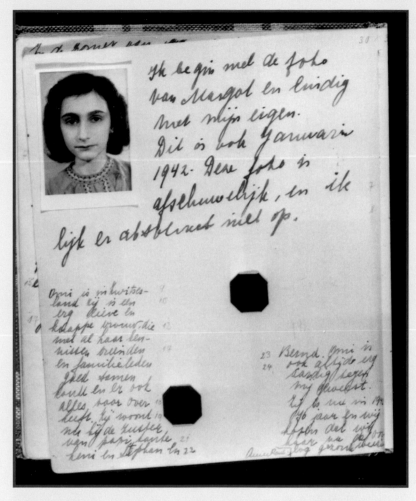

■ Anne Frank wrote in her diary as if she were talking to a friend: "I hope I will be able to confide everything to you, as I have never been able to confide in anyone, and I hope you will be a great source of comfort and support."

■ Peter van Pels (pictured here and called van Daan in the *Diary*) and his parents were in hiding with the Franks. The developing romance between Anne Frank and Peter features prominently in the *Diary*.

■ Anne adored her father, Otto Frank (right), but had a more difficult relationship with her mother, Edith Frank (left). After the war, it was Otto who helped bring about the publication of Anne's diary.

■ Herman (left) and Auguste van Pels (right)—referred to as Mr. and Mrs. van Daan in the *Diary*—along with their son, Peter, were a Jewish family in hiding with the Franks. Both of them died in German concentration camps.

■ Fritz Pfeffer—called Albert Dussel in the *Diary*—was a dentist who joined the group in the Secret Annex shortly after they went into hiding.

■ Johannes Kleiman (left) and Victor Kugler (right) were two
of the helpers who protected the Franks and others in the Secret
Annex, at great danger to themselves. They were also arrested
and imprisoned, but both survived the war.

■ Miep Gies (seated) and Bep Voskuijl (Ellie) helped those in hiding by bringing them food, clothing, and news of the outside world. It was Miep Gies who found and preserved Anne's diary.

■ The building at 263 Prinsengracht in Amsterdam (pictured above) housed the offices of Otto Frank's business, Opteka. In the back, on the top two floors and in the attic, was the Secret Annex. Today, it is a museum dedicated to Anne Frank.

■ After their arrest, Anne Frank and the others in hiding were herded together with many other Jews and transported to concentration camps in Poland. Otto Frank was the only survivor.

J

3

The Plot

THE DIMENSIONS OF THE PLOT

USUALLY A DIARY is a daily narrative account of the diarist's experiences, thoughts, and feelings. It is not expected to have a plot (story plan). It presents, rather, the diarist's responses to the events of the day. It can be full of anecdotes and incidents, so patterns of thought and behavior are bound to emerge. Since a diary is usually a private record, the diarist hardly needs to tell a story already familiar to herself. Rather than being unified by a plot, a diary is held together by the personality of the author and the circumstances of her life that she chooses to write down. The plot, such as it is, of Anne Frank's *Diary* grows out of, and *is*, the reaction to the circumstances that confront her and the others in hiding with her.

Anne began her diary as a private exercise for her own purposes:

> Writing in a diary is a really strange experience for someone like me. Not only because I've never written anything before, but also because it seems to me that later on neither I nor anyone else will be interested in the musings of a thirteen-year-old schoolgirl. Oh well, it doesn't matter. I feel like writing, and I have an even greater need to get all kinds of things off my chest.[16]

In this entry Anne contemplates a saying "paper has more patience than people"—a saying she thought of one day while sitting inside brooding. Following this brief contemplation, Anne moves on to the point that she writes because she has no one to confide in. She humorously suggests that she has "a throng of admirers" and that on the surface, she is not wanting in her relationships, but insists that she lacks a "true friend." She admits that with her friends, unlike in a diary, she cannot get much beyond talking about everyday things.

Keeping a diary was to be a way to explore herself and to get things off her chest because Anne felt, she said, that she had no one she could really open up to despite her general appearance of being outgoing. Her feelings, relationships, and conflicts, thus, form the plot of the diary.

But the historical and political situation surrounding its composition gives the plot of Anne's *Diary* another dimension. It is not only going to be an exercise in self discovery but a witness to a historical tragedy and the way a set of people respond to, bear, and succumb to that tragedy.

Additionally, because the plot of Anne's *Diary* is not all within the text itself but involves the story of the diary's composition and the fate of its author, the reader must participate in the construction of the plot by knowledge of events that Anne could not know, such as the eventual raid of the Secret Annex, the extermination of seven of its eight inhabitants, and the ultimate publication of the *Diary*. These events could not enter into her strategy as a writer since the story of the Secret Annex unfolded for her as she wrote about it. When the climax came, she was in no position to describe it.

The Diary of Anne Frank, then, in addition to being what she originally intended it to be—a friend and confidant—tells the story of a Jewish girl hiding from the Nazis who kept a journal portraying what it was like to be a Jewish girl in hiding. As well as mapping her own growth, Anne described what it was like to live as a fugitive, what the people she was in hiding with were like, how they responded to confinement, how they occupied themselves, how they interacted with each other, and how she got along with each of them.

ON YOUR OWN
ACTIVITY #6

The plot of Anne Frank's *Diary* depends on how people respond to a series of usually catastrophic or nearly catastrophic events as well as some relatively minor but irritating, or even comical, daily events. Recall and describe some of the events recorded in Anne Frank's *Diary* and describe how the people involved respond to them and interact with each other in those situations.

A MAP OF THE PLOT

At the start of her diary, before Anne transformed her entries into letters to Kitty, she recapitulated her family's situation, the rise of German fascism, and the consequent plight of Jews. That account appears in the first section of the diary, covering the brief period before Anne and her family went into hiding. She wrote about her friends, going to school, playing ping-pong, going to the ice-cream parlor, flirting with boys, and about the difficulties Jews were facing under Nazi rule. The section ends with the entry of Sunday, July 5, 1942. At this point in the diary, a succession of anecdotes gives way to a movement of plot: because of Nazi terror, the Franks go into hiding. These are the last words Anne wrote before going into hiding:

> "But when, Father?" He sounded so serious that I got scared.
>
> "Don't you worry. We'll take care of everything. Just enjoy your carefree life while you can."
>
> That was it. Oh, may these somber words not come true for as long as possible.
>
> The doorbell's ringing, Hello's [Hello is the nickname of a Dutch boy who likes Anne] here, time to stop.[17]

When Anne made her next entry, on the following Wednesday, July 8, the family was in hiding, and they would be for the remainder of the diary.

Characteristically, Anne writes in an easy manner, as if she were speaking, despite the important fact that "the whole world [has] turned upside down," and it has become normal to say: "I'm still alive, and that's the main thing." Although it is the main thing for Anne and her comrades in hiding, it is not the main subject of Anne's diary. It is only the inescapable background of the diary against which everything else occurs. That in itself is remarkable. The primary plot of the diary involves the way Anne interacts with the others in the Secret Annex, her own reflections on her behavior, and the way she grows over the two years the diary covers.

As we examine the plot of Anne Frank's *Diary* and trace "what happens," it may be useful to borrow two terms from the Greek philosopher Aristotle's analysis of drama in *The Poetics*: *recognition* and *reversal*. Much of the action of Anne's diary is the action of consciousness, especially her consciousness or self-awareness. Consciousness is primarily a matter of recognition, the kind of insight that is the result of or leads to change of some kind. It follows or leads to a reversal in a life situation or in the way we look at or understand things, events, or people. Recognizing something is itself an action. In examining the plot of Anne's diary, then, we ought to notice what recognitions her experience brings to her and how those recognitions affect her growth.

The story that Anne's diary tells begins with Otto Frank's recognition that life has taken a fundamentally bad turn. His awareness of a reversal, the Nazi invasion of Holland, leads him to respond to the threat by setting in motion the plans to go into hiding in order to evade captivity, deportation, and death. The story Anne tells in her diary begins with this reversal. As Anne writes, the world has suddenly been turned upside down. The Nazi invasion begins a reversal (a change for the worse) for her life. She goes from being a free and active girl who attends school and plays with friends to being a confined and endangered creature living in continuous proximity to seven others, also threatened and confined, five of them adults.

Life in confinement is the living condition for the rest of the diary. Anne narrates the move from relative freedom to the confinement of hiding with a picture both comic and heartbreaking: "So there we were, Father, Mother and I, walking in the pouring rain, each of us with a schoolbag and a shopping bag filled to the brim with the most varied assortment of items." Even here, at such a time, when she is leaving her entire life behind her and is in mortal danger, Anne is able to take in the environment around her in detail: "The people on their way to work at that early hour gave us sympathetic looks; you could tell by their faces that they were sorry they couldn't offer us some kind of transportation; the conspicuous yellow star spoke for itself."[18]

Her ability to see the environment around her and to recreate it in writing enabled Anne to hold on to her sense of self even when she had to abandon her past. By telling her story, Anne controlled the story, despite the reality that the story was really controlling her. Her diary is an educational romance or *bildungsroman*, a story organized around the maturing of the main character's perceptions, which shows her psychological development. The tragic irony in Anne's case is that this development, because of the immediate circumstances of Nazi persecution, counted for nothing in her immediate life. It could not keep her physically alive. Whether she grew in wisdom and fortitude or not, Anne's end was the same: a wretched death from typhus (a deadly bacterial disease) in the Bergen-Belsen concentration camp. But this irony is undermined by the fact that the diary survived and, therefore, Anne's growth and self-awareness do matter as literature, testimony, and inspiration. Her death was not obliteration but transformation. The diary assured the continued life of Anne's spirit. The completion of the plot and the continuation of her life depend as much on the reader as they do on the author: our reading the *Diary* and remembering Anne make up one of the climaxes of the plot.

The plot of the middle section of Anne's diary is woven out of several strands. However, the principal and encompassing action is not concluded in the diary's narrative: the hopeful effort of the eight Jews in hiding to outlive the reign of their persecutors and emerge from hiding after the Nazis have been defeated. This effort is always in the background and is repeatedly revealed when the safety of the Secret Annex is threatened by burglaries, inspections by a new landlord, or Allied aerial bombardment, as well as by the attempts to live daily as normally as possible. Surrounding this plot is the story of the war itself and its worldwide effects. Connected to these plot strands is the story of a girl who writes a diary about her life under these circumstances and the story of the diary's fate once the diarist is captured.

Anne's description of the effects of the occupation and the war on the people of Amsterdam comes from reports of the news that the helpers bring—years later, in her account of Anne's life, Miep Gies reported that Anne always welcomed her when she visited by saying, "Hello, Miep, and what is the news?"—and from the few furtive fugitive glances Anne got out the attic window. She presented these threads of plot with such descriptive immediacy that it seems she is an on-the-spot reporter rather than a girl in hiding.

One such harrowing report is from January 13, 1943 in which Anne writes, "...poor helpless people are being dragged out of their homes.... Families are torn apart; men, women and children are separated." She continues describing the scene "Everyone is scared. Every night hundreds of planes pass over Holland on their way to German cities, to sow their bombs on German soil."[19] In the midst of this report, however, Anne quickly shifts the focus and dramatically contrasts these events with life in the Secret Annex. she writes, "As for us, we're quite fortunate. Luckier than millions of people. It's quite safe here, and we're using our money to buy food."[20]

For the reader who knows what Anne cannot—that there will be no "after the war" for her—her words have a depth beyond the humanity they reflect. Similarly, the final sentence of this entry foreshadows an end unknown to Anne: "All we can do is wait, as calmly as possible, for it to end. Jews and Christians are waiting, the whole world is waiting, and many are waiting for death."[21] Implicit is the unspoken phrase, "without their knowing it." And the poignancy and power of her diary is that Anne is among those who wait.

Within the framework of this situation, there are several plot strands. Some involve Anne's accounts of the interactions of the characters with whom she lives. We have already seen the kind of bickering the van Daans engage in with each other, and Anne reports conflicts over food and space as well as attacks of jealousy. We see the conflicts between Anne and Mr. Dussel with whom she is forced to share a room and a work desk. We share Anne's frustrations and insights as Anne herself even grew tired of telling these stories, as in the entry for January 15, 1944.

In this entry, Anne moved from describing external situations to a poignant glimpse at her inner self, and in later entries she revealed her hopes, regrets, and longings, partly through stories of past friendships and romances, and partly through descriptions of the physical and psychological changes she was undergoing as she entered womanhood.

The principal events for Anne in the Secret Annex were the romance that developed between her and Peter, her parents' reaction, and her responses to her feelings about Peter's character and her parents' disapproval of the amount of time they spent alone together. All of these events—bodily changes, longing, romance, conflicts with parents—are quite common, but because they happen under the extreme circumstances recounted in the diary, they are filled with added drama.

When Anne and Peter are thrown together in the Secret Annex, Anne finds nothing attractive about him, although a reader may suspect that, under the circumstances, they will be drawn together, much as they would be as characters in a novel. At first, Anne finds Peter to be withdrawn and lazy, and she suspects he does not like her since she seems to be his opposite, full of energy and talkative, even to the point of seeming brash and rude. Her unrelenting liveliness, in fact, brings reproaches upon her from the grown-ups. What Anne and Peter do have in common is youth, confinement, and the need for a caring, understanding connection with another person, in order to discover not only the hidden person in the other but the deeper person in oneself.

The change in Anne's attitude toward Peter begins with changes in herself: "Whenever anyone used to speak of sexual problems at home or at school, it was either something mysterious or revolting."[22] But at the end of 1943, Anne began menstruating and developing breasts. "I think what is happening to me is so wonderful," she wrote on January 5, 1944, "and not only what can be seen on my body, but all that is taking place inside."[23]

Readers can see in this entry what makes Anne the powerful writer she is despite her youth and inexperience. It is her forthright ability to speak openly and without shame about everything, to be a detached observer of events which, nevertheless, deeply involve her. Rather than judging or repressing, she describes, and in the process affords readers insight into common human consciousness as well as into the human experience at a particularly stressful time in history. Anne continues in this entry to explore and express her feelings—she is alive, despite everything, and feels herself growing, and takes pleasure in that experience—with an openness that may at first be shocking but that has the innocent wonder of a creature beholding unknown elements of her world. (It must be noted, too, that this is a section of Anne's diary that Otto Frank allowed to be included in the edited version of the diary he published after the war.)

In this passage she questions some of the feelings she knew lurked inside of her on the subconscious level. She openly talks of how once she had the desire to kiss another girl, and that she did so. She tells of how she was inquisitive of the other girl's body, and states that she goes into

ON YOUR OWN
ACTIVITY #7

Many stories of individual experiences during the Holocaust have been written by survivors of the Holocaust, among them Elie Wiesel's *Night* and Lore Segal's *Other People's Houses*. At the web address *www.remember.org/bksrvr.html* you will find a list of many other such works. Choose from among these books, or others that you find through your own research, and write a short essay comparing and contrasting Anne Frank's story with the other story you read.

ecstasies when she sees the naked female figure, such as Venus. She also speaks of how wonderful and exquisite she finds the female form—so much so that it brings tears to her eyes. Presented in a straightforward and inquisitive manner, the reader is allowed an intimate glimpse of Anne as she considers her own sexuality.[24]

In this state of curiosity and wonder about sexuality and being a woman, Anne begins her friendship with Peter: "My longing to talk to someone became so intense that somehow or other I took it into my head to choose Peter."[25] For Anne, it may be the vague "somehow or other." The attentive reader, however, has followed her confessions well enough to know that Anne lacks confidence in her mother and holds back from sharing intimate experiences with her, that she feels uncomfortable talking about intimate female experiences with her father despite her devotion to him, and that although she and her sister Margot are friendly, they are not close. Moreover, Peter van Daan shares the name Peter with a boy in school Anne had a crush on, Peter Wessel, and this coincidence gives him a certain luster.

Anne's first moment of intimacy with Peter van Daan comes as they sit facing each other as he does a crossword puzzle. With her writer's sensitivity, she sees what she had not seen before, "... on his face, that look of helplessness and uncertainty as to how to behave..."[26]

Slowly, after this moment, their intimacy develops through several encounters around everyday matters. They become more open with each other. In a conversation with Peter and Margot, Anne expresses confusion about the gender of the warehouse cat, Boche. Peter says it is male, but Anne thinks that the cat is pregnant because of a swelling in its body (which is really the result of a bone inflammation).

Peter goes into the warehouse after hours when it is safe to venture there and "picked up the animal, turned him over on his back, deftly held his head and paws together, and the lesson began."[27] In her diary entry of January 24, 1944, Anne tells of how Peter was able to prove the cat's sex and continue talking normally without any unpleasantness. This matter-of-fact approach allowed her to feel at ease.[28]

After this, situations within the Secret Annex, which, before their developing interest in each other, would not have, now bring them together. Peter helps Anne search for good potatoes in the barrel in the attic, and when she has to pass through his room to get more potatoes, they start talking about studying French and then about Peter's feelings about being Jewish. Anne begins to realize that Peter "needs some affection, too, of course,"[29] just as she does. And "[w]henever I go upstairs now I keep on hoping that I shall see 'him.' Because my life now has an object, and I have something to look forward to, everything has become more pleasant."[30]

Having Anne's sympathy, Peter begins to open up to her. In her entry for February 14, 1944, Anne writes of an argument between Peter and Mr. Dussel that resulted in Peter's losing his temper. Disturbed by his reaction, Peter unburdens himself to Anne the next day, telling her how hard it is for him to speak when he is angry and how he simply wants to "get to work with [his] fists." But he "realize[s] this method does not get me anywhere," he tells her, and adds, "That is why I admire you. You are never at a loss for words, you say exactly what you want to say to people and are never the least bit shy."[31]

Anne confesses it is not so, and then sits on the floor, glad to have a renewed sense of fellowship, not unlike what she had experienced with her girlfriends.[32] Anne's feeling of fellowship with Peter grows into a tender sympathy for him, which strongly reflects her own need for someone to be attentive to her, whom she cares for and who cares for her. In a sense, Peter becomes someone on whom she can lavish the tenderness she herself craves.

It is from this tension within her that the love story between Anne and Peter develops. It is a story tinged not only with the common emotional needs of adolescent longing but amplified by the constant pressure of confinement in the Secret Annex and the terror of the Nazi threat. In her entry of February 19, 1944, a Saturday, when the building was empty, allowing those in hiding to enjoy more freedom of movement within it, Anne wrote:

> I went to the private office, with my blanket and every-thing, to sit at the desk and read or write. It was not long before it all became too much for me, my head drooped on to my arm, and I sobbed my heart out. The tears streamed down my cheeks and I felt desperately unhappy. Oh, if only "he" had come to comfort me...

Anne tells of how she went upstairs again hoping to run into Peter, and that when the chance meeting did not occur, and instead he went to the warehouse to see Boche the cat, she began to cry again, feeling "very wretched." She explains what was going through her mind saying, "Who knows, perhaps he doesn't even like me at all and doesn't need anyone to confide in. Perhaps he only thinks about me in a casual sort of way."[33]

Anne's highly charged doubt about the depth of Peter's love for her is also a way of expressing and discharging the tension developed from living the kind of life forced upon her by the Nazis and the stoical, even cheerful endurance it demands. At least when longing for Peter is the focus of her anguish, it is a self torment that can find relief. A few days later, Anne stands beside Peter in the attic: "He stood with his head against a thick beam, and I sat down. We breathed the fresh air, looked outside, and both felt that the spell should not be broken by words."[34]

The story of Anne's romance with Peter does not play out as it might in a novel. A reader who wishes to see its full development will be disappointed. It has no more status of place in Anne's diary than accounts of potato peeling, warehouse break-ins, or news about Allied (the nations fighting Germany) victories and responses to them by the inmates of the Secret Annex. We learn that the relationship becomes sexual for them but not to what degree, that Anne's parents object to it, and that Anne lessens its intensity but does not stop spending time alone with Peter. The part of the story of Anne and Peter that we as readers encounter most often, however, is Anne's thoughts about that relationship. She often does not set down details—after all, she knows them—but reflects upon them. The drama of Anne's romance with Peter, as she narrates it, is far more her internal, psychological quest than the story of their actual relationship. Thus, she writes entries like the one for Wednesday, 14 June, 1944 in which she states, "Peter loves me not as a lover but as a friend and grows more affectionate every day. But what is the mysterious something that holds me back?"[35] In this same entry she describes Peter as being good and peace-loving, but she also states that there is a lot about him that disappoints her. Though she has no answers, Anne questions why Peter is so closed-off, and speculates that he must still long for someone to confide in.

Another good example of Anne's internal struggle over her relationship with Peter can be found in her entry for July 15, 1944. In this entry Anne states that it was she who conquered and won over Peter as opposed to it being the other way around, but she seems to regret letting the relationship develop the way it had. She suspects that she may have drawn Peter in too closely, and that now she does not have the type of friendship that she had hoped to develop. Anne states that she needed a person to whom she could pour her heart out, and that when she achieved that, her relationship with Peter automatically developed more intimately. She recognizes that she should have explored other possibilities, and she sees the satisfaction he gets from their meetings. Unfortunately, she feels that he clings to her, and that she won't be able to shake him free or help him stand on his own.[36]

The story of Anne's psychological debates and development, which unfolds through her interaction with Peter, her father and mother, the van Daans, and Mr. Dussel, is given a tragic dimension because of the war. The

ON YOUR OWN
ACTIVITY #8

Anne's *Diary* is considered a complete work, and certainly, knowing the outcome of the events creates both a sense of closure and poignancy to her last entry. Consider some of the many things Anne did not get to experience, and some of the tales that she did not get a chance to tell. What do you suppose other entries might have looked like, how do you think her relationship with Peter might have developed? Though it is difficult to speculate, would her diary have lost some of it's power and immediacy were Anne to have survived the Holocaust and been able to publish the work herself?

terrible irony is that the mood of political hope is strong toward the end of Anne's diary. Anne gives a graphic account of D-day, June 6, 1944, the day of the Normandy landing—the Allied invasion of Europe—citing news from both English and German radio broadcasts, and finishing the entry for that day with a description of the response in the Secret Annex.[37]

There is real cause for hope, for the war will soon be over, the Allies victorious, and the oppressed liberated, except for the millions who were its victims. However, in what would have been the final days of hiding before liberation, the inhabitants of the Secret Annex were betrayed and arrested. But that story, of course, cannot be included in Anne's entries. (And we still don't know who betrayed them.) Her diary ends with what would have constituted her continuing quest to know and define herself, in a world full of other people who might never understand her completely, just as the Nazis were unable to see Jews in their human completeness. Even Anne's inner musings about her own nature may be a metaphorical meditation on her historical dilemma:

> [T]he prospect that I may be sitting on school benches next October makes me feel far too cheerful to be logical! ... hadn't I just told you that I didn't want to be too hopeful? Forgive me, they haven't given me the name "little bundle of contradictions" all for nothing! ...
>
> A voice sobs within me: "There you are, that's what's become of you: you're uncharitable, you look supercilious and peevish, people dislike you and all because you won't listen to the advice given you by your own better half." Oh, I

would like to listen, but it doesn't work; if I'm quiet and serious, everyone thinks it's a new comedy and then I have to get out of it by turning it into a joke, not to mention my own family, who are sure to think I'm ill, make me swallow pills for headaches and nerves, feel my neck and my head to see whether I'm running a temperature, ask if I'm constipated and criticize me for being in a bad mood. I can't keep that up: if I'm watched to that extent, I start by getting snappy, then unhappy, and finally I twist my heart round again, so that the bad is on the outside and the good is on the inside and keep on trying to find a way of becoming what I would so like to be, and what I could be, if ... there weren't any other people living in the world.[38]

Characters and Characterization

ANNE

TO KEEP A DIARY, to set down and examine everything that happens to you and that you experience, you need to have a rather strong sense of yourself, and Anne did. Yet, she was not conceited. She knew her strength, as indicated in her entry for Saturday, 15 July, 1944: "I have one outstanding trait, that is my knowledge of myself."[39] Her focus on herself was a discipline she practiced in order to make sure she was a good and righteous person. She was introspective as well as outgoing. She was self-assured yet always ready to question herself. She was vulnerable and strong, flexible and uncompromising. She called herself a little bundle of contradictions. Moreover, as focused as she was on herself, that focus did not prevent concern for or identification with others. "I feel wicked," she wrote, "sleeping in a warm bed, while my dearest friends have been knocked down or have fallen into the gutter somewhere out in the cold night."[40] Anne was set on being good and in her entry for July 6, 1944 she maps out a method for self-improvement. Here she suggests that everybody should spend some time before falling asleep in the evening trying to recall the events of the day, and reflect on what has been bad and good saying, "Then, without realizing it, you try to improve yourself at the start of each new day."[41]

It seems she was also describing what she did daily as a writer and showing also what for her must have formed the moral dimension of writing.

The vitality of Anne Frank's *Diary* comes perhaps more from the vivid sketches of the people with whom she inhabited the Secret Annex than from a richly developed plot, for the plot of Anne's diary depends on the nature and situation of the characters she describes. Although made up of a series of unified anecdotes of conflicts and resolutions, and overshadowed by the historical events that generate Anne's story, Anne Frank's *Diary* at its core is a collection of character sketches.

Anne herself is, of course, the main character in her diary, and by its end she is a living, breathing figure. The reader knows Anne from having spent a good deal of time with her, not just experiencing the scenes she described, but seeing her probe her own consciousness and motives as well as the thoughts and actions of the others in the Secret Annex. Because we are reading Anne's diary, our sense of each character is, of course, set by Anne's viewpoint, and in each case Anne's sense of a character not only reveals something about that person but adds to our view of Anne herself. Moreover, characters become known to us primarily as Anne perceived them and as they interacted with her.

OTTO FRANK

Otto Frank was the engineer of the plan to hide in the secret Annex. Anne wrote that her father had had a heart-breaking first love before his marriage, and he is presented as self disciplined, a perfectionist, calm, and thoughtful. He is a dedicated father, both permissive and stern. He places a high value on learning and orderliness. Not only does he help Anne and Margot with their studies, but he takes correspondence courses himself. Anne adores and respects him. She also feels that he is emotionally remote from her, that he does not really understand her, and that in order for her to grow, she must assert herself, even if it means going against his wishes, as in the matter of what he terms "necking" with Peter. Perhaps the reader gets the best sense of

ON YOUR OWN
ACTIVITY #9

Of all the people hiding in the Secret Annex, only Anne's father Otto Frank survived the Nazi death camps. After the liberation, Otto returned to Amsterdam and lived with Miep Gies and her husband for seven years. Using what you know of Otto's character from Anne's diary, and after learning more about Miep Gies by researching her on the Internet, write a dialogue between Miep Gies and Otto in which they remember and discuss the years in hiding and all the people they have lost.

Otto's character in Anne's letter to him, included in the diary, regarding her relationship with Peter.

Anne's is a strong letter, which might test any parent. Otto's reaction in the immediate situation is not tempered by an appreciation that Anne is in the process of trying to become herself, independent yet morally accountable to her own sense of right and wrong. He shames her by casting her in the role of an ungrateful child.

And she does feel ashamed. But this is not Otto's final response to Anne's self-assertive letter, for it was he who helped bring about its publication in the *Diary*.

EDITH FRANK

Anne's mother, Edith Frank, is a less vivid presence in the diary than Anne's father. Whereas Anne was strongly attached to her father emotionally, and part of the process of her growth involved distancing herself from his influence, she felt herself emotionally alienated from her mother and different from her from the outset. "I'm the opposite of Mother, so of course we clash," Anne wrote on November 7, 1942.[42] In one entry, Anne described her longing for her mother's affection: "I longed for her to look lovingly at me." Instead, her mother "made some remark or other that seemed unfriendly."[43] Anne felt that her mother had no appreciation of her emotional needs, and she held that against her.

Anne also saw herself as different from her mother in the way they coped with unhappiness. According to Anne, her mother's "counsel when one feels melancholy is: 'think of all the misery in the world and be thankful that you are not sharing in it!' My advice is: 'Go outside, to the fields, enjoy nature and the sunshine, go out and try to recapture happiness in yourself and in God. Think of all the beauty that's still left in and around you and be happy!'"[44]

PETER VAN DAAN

From Anne's descriptions of him, Peter van Daan emerges as a warm, generous, and sweet-tempered boy, courageous and gallant, but also shy, quiet, introspective, in need of affection, and without the moral focus and determination that drives Anne. "His dislike of religion" does not "appeal" to her, and "it strikes fear to [her] heart when Peter talks of ... being a criminal, or of gambling," when he grows up. "Although it's meant as a joke," Anne wrote, "it gives me the feeling that he's afraid of his own weakness."[45] He can spend hours alone in the warehouse playing with the cat, and he can dress up in one of his mother's dresses as Anne wears one of his suits to entertain the others in the Secret Annex.

Anne wrote that she had wooed and conquered him, but in her narration of events, Peter seems, at times, to be the one who put himself forward and wooed her: "Whenever he looks at me with those eyes, with that smile and that wink, it's as if a light goes on inside me."[46] "This morning Peter asked me if I'd come again one evening. He swore I wouldn't be disturbing him, and said that where there was room for one, there was room for two."[47]

MR. AND MRS. VAN DAAN AND MR. DUSSEL

Living as a group, confined and fearful in small quarters with scarce resources and without knowing how long confinement will last, requires of each group member a sense of cooperation and awareness. It is almost inevitable in this kind of situation to have at least one person who is unable to see that the needs of the group must come first and whose selfishness causes difficulties. In the Secret Annex, Mr. Dussel and Mrs. van Daan both represent this sort of character. Anne saw Mr. Dussel as a man who puts his own interests first and Mrs. van Daan as a relatively hysterical and short-sighted woman—vain, flirtatious, opinionated, and quarrelsome. Toward the end of their time in the Secret Annex, in her entry for Friday, 16 June, 1944, Anne offered a thumbnail sketch of Mrs. van Daan and her effect on the others. [48]

Mr. Dussel, a dentist invited to join the group in the Secret Annex a short time after they had gone into hiding, has a non-Jewish girlfriend, and although it is risky and thus not in the best interest of the group in hiding, he has the helpers deliver letters to his lady-love. When he receives "eggs, butter, cookies, lemonade, bread, cognac, spice cake, oranges, chocolate, books, and writing paper" from her on his birthday—things not easily attainable on the outside, either—he displays them, but refuses to share them. Anne notes, furthermore, that "[w]e found bread, cheese, jam and eggs in his cupboard." She comments, "It's disgraceful that Dussel, whom we've treated with such kindness and whom we took in to save from destruction, should stuff himself behind our backs and not give us anything."[49] Until Dussel moved in, Anne had a room to herself. When he arrived, she had to share the room with him and sleep on a makeshift bed, extended to her length by a chair added to the foot of her couch. Her entry for July 13, 1943, details the story of her winning some time to work at the desk in her room after Dussel high-handedly refused even to consider sharing the desk with her.[50]

Mr. van Daan is a rather nondescript character, a quiet, intelligent man harried by his wife and subject to her moods. His primary enjoyment seems to be smoking tobacco.

MARGOT FRANK

Anne's sister, Margot Frank, is hardly a fully developed character. She appears to be less extroverted than Anne, is a good student, and unlike Anne, her relationship with her mother is an easy one. The nature of the relationship between the sisters and the way it developed, as seen from Anne's point of view, is suggested by an entry from January 12, 1944: "Margot has grown so sweet; she seems quite different from what she used to be, isn't nearly so catty these days and is becoming a real friend. Nor does she regard me as a little kid who counts for nothing."[51]

When Anne became close with Peter, she worried that Margot could feel excluded, and the two exchanged letters in which Margot assured Anne that, "I'm jealous of neither you nor Peter." Yet in those letters, she continued to show a bit of the sisterly cattiness that Anne had referred to earlier.[52] The bitter irony, again, is that, whatever their characters, whatever their consuming interests and disturbing conflicts or burning desires, all eight of these people were stripped of their identities by the Nazis and turned into part of a mass to be exterminated. By her *Diary*, Anne contributed an important counterforce, despite the deaths, against that massive dehumanization.

THEIR PROTECTORS

Woven throughout Anne's narrative are a group of Dutch people—particularly Miep and Jan Gies (called Henk), Johannes Kleiman (called Mr. Koophuis), Victor Kugler (called Mr. Kraler), and Bep Voskuijl (called Elli)—who helped the eight Jews in hiding, sustaining them both materially and spiritually, bringing news of the outside world, food, clothing, and even little gifts when they could, despite the terrible dangers involved and the difficulties in their own lives: "Mr. Kraler has been called up to go digging [to perform forced labor for the Nazis]. Elli has a streaming cold and will probably have to stay at home tomorrow. Miep hasn't fully recovered from her flu yet, and Koophuis has had such bad hemorrhage of the stomach that he lost consciousness."[53] They come across as a group of decent, human, steadfast, and loyal souls, heroic without even trying to be heroes. These words of Miep Gies, spoken years later, characterize all of them:

> My decision to help Otto was because I saw no alternative. I could foresee many sleepless nights and an unhappy life if I refused. And that was not the kind of failure I wanted for myself. Permanent remorse about failing to do your human duty, in my opinion, can be worse than losing your life.[54]

The Setting:
The Secret Annex

NEARLY ALL OF THE ACTION of Anne Frank's *Diary* takes place within the confines of the Secret Annex, a set of rooms on three floors at the back of an old canal-side building at 263 Prinsengracht in Amsterdam, where Anne, her family, and the others were hiding. The building housed the offices of Otto Frank's and Mr. van Daan's business, Opekta, and, in a manner of speaking, the Franks and their friends were hiding right out in the open, almost as if they were hiding in their own home. The layout of the building allowed for this as did the cover story of

their escape that Otto established before going to the building on Prinsengracht. The van Daans arrived at the hiding
place a week after the Franks, and Anne used Mr. van
Daan's account to inform us of Otto's strategy for estab-
lishing the alibi. From Mr. van Daan's account we learn
that Mr. Goudsmit found a letter that was left behind by the
Franks, and that as he and Mr. van Daan were tidying up,
Mr. van Daan pretended to be surprised at finding a notepad
with an address in Maastricht, Belgium written on it. Mr.
van Daan then pretended to recall that Mr. Frank had been
visited by a high-ranking officer stationed in Maastricht
who had offered to help the Franks. We know that the ploy
worked because as he concludes his retelling he states,
"Most of your friends know already [that you've gone to
Maastricht], because I've been told myself several times by
different people."[55]

The building at 263 Prinsengracht still stands. It is a tall
narrow building, part of a row, with buildings touching it on
either side.

A large warehouse occupied the ground floor, which was
also used as a store and a workroom where spices were
milled and ground. Next to the door to the warehouse/store
was the door to the house. This door opened on to a second
door, which led to a staircase. At the top of the staircase
was another door with a frosted glass panel, which opened
into a large office with several smaller rooms, a cupboard,
a safe, and the director's office. A passage led past a coal
storage room; up a few steps was the showroom. That was
the first floor, as it is called in Europe, although an American would call it the second floor.

From the ground floor, there was another steep staircase
leading to the floor above the one just described. There

were several rooms on this floor and a passage to the front part of the attic. But to the right of the landing, there was a plain gray door. Beyond that door, there was another steep staircase that led to the three floors of rooms at the back of the building—two floors and the rear attic—that became the Secret Annex. The gray door leading to this complex was hidden by a bookcase that covered it but could swing open when the hook that held it against the door was unfastened.

Most of the time, the secret inhabitants of 263 Prinsengracht were confined to the space behind the gray door hidden by the bookcase. During the day, when the building was in use as a business headquarters, they had to keep silent, refrain from running water or flushing the toilet and sometimes even moving around. Nighttimes and weekends, when the building was empty, they enjoyed greater

ON YOUR OWN
ACTIVITY #10

Although Anne Frank's *Diary* is set almost entirely within the small space of the Secret Annex, the events of the outside world, from which the Jews in hiding are entirely cut off physically, are ever present in the Annex. After some research using the Internet, the library, or interviews with friends and relatives who may have lived through that time, describe some aspects of the world outside the Secret Annex, during the years 1942–1944, focusing, as you choose, on the political setting, the military setting, or what daily life was like for non-Jews living in one of the Nazi-occupied countries or for people living in one of the unoccupied but resisting countries like England or the United States.

freedom of movement and might use the offices and the warehouse, careful always to leave no sign that they had been there.

Space in the Secret Annex was scarce, and the sense of confinement was extreme. The inhabitants lived with little privacy and seldom were they even able to open a window. Anne compared herself "to a songbird whose wings have been ripped off and who keeps hurling itself against the bars of its dark cage."[56] Several days later, Anne wrote this impression of life in the Secret Annex:

> I see the eight of us with our "Secret Annex" as if we were a little piece of blue heaven, surrounded by heavy black rain clouds. The round, clearly defined spot where we stand is still safe, but the clouds gather more closely about us and the circle which separates us from the approaching danger closes more and more tightly[57]

What might be surprising for readers of Anne's *Diary* is that we do not come away with a sense of claustrophobia despite the pent-up conditions Anne described. This is probably because her wish to transcend her life—to

ON YOUR OWN
ACTIVITY #11

Anne Frank's *Diary* was turned into a play, *The Diary of Anne Frank*, in 1956 by Frances Goodrich and Albert Hackett. In 1997, Wendy Kesselman revised their adaptation to reflect the additional material published in The Critical Edition of Anne Frank's *Diary*. After reading either the original adaptation or the revised version, write a short essay examining the ways the adaptors transferred the setting of the diary from the page to the stage.

live after her death, achieved through writing her diary—was fulfilled as well with regard to the space in which she lived, for the amplitude of her environment is a function not of the narrowness of her physical surroundings but of the breadth of consciousness that her diary shows.

6

Themes and Symbols in Anne Frank's *Diary*

A SYMBOL IS SOMETHING with a meaning or identity of its own that can stand for or represent something else. A house, for example, may represent warmth, domestic activities, security, achievement, etc., depending upon the context. In literature, symbols help enlarge the subject that the author is writing about, providing dimension to what otherwise might be flat. Symbols can give depth to what might be shallow and meaning to what might be ordinary. A writer employs symbolism deliberately to make connections between several aspects of a work and, thus, to contribute to the artistic unity

55

of the work. Symbols help make a story coherent: often one event is foreshadowed, or announced, by an earlier event that, because of its relation to the later event, becomes symbolic of it.

An example of such symbolic foreshadowing occurs in Anne Frank's *Diary* in the entry for November 11, 1943, which she called, "Ode to My Fountain Pen: In Memoriam." In the entry, Anne described how her fountain pen, unseen by anyone, fell off her writing table, was swept up with the dirt of the floor, and burned with the garbage in the stove. The incident is ordinary enough. In her telling it, Anne did not give the incident more emotion than it was worth, and the tone she uses is light. She described the pen, pointed to its virtues, and told of the time she got it (she was nine, had the flu, and the winds were blowing outside). She described her years of use and how some teachers let her write with it in school, but others insisted that everyone use the school pens and ink pots. Characteristically, Anne

ON YOUR OWN
ACTIVITY #12

When we think of real, living, flesh and blood people, we try not to think of them as symbols signifying ideas or abstractions or anything but themselves in all the complexity and with all the contradictions of humanity—although we sometimes do. The Nazis, however, were determined not to see Jews as individuals but as symbols, as representing ideas, types, and characteristics. After some research, write a short essay about what Jews represented inside the Nazi way of thinking and why you think the Nazis might have seen, or needed to see, Jews that way.

was able to use writing about the pen as a means of writing about herself and the world she lived in. When she finished recounting the history of her pen and her relation to it, Anne goes into great detail describing the circumstances of how she lost it. Having been forced to make room for her father and Margot, Anne set the pen down and began rubbing beans (in order to remove mold from them). She swept the floor and dumped the dirt, along with the rotten beans into the fire. She recounts, "A giant flame shot up, and I thought it was wonderful that the stove which had been gasping its last breath, had made such a miraculous recovery." When Anne returned to the table to continue her writing, she could not find her pen, and though everyone helped to look for the pen, it was not found. The next day when her father went to empty the stove, the gold clip from the pen was discovered among the ashes. Anne concluded, "I'm left with one consolation, small though it may be: my fountain pen was cremated, just as I would like to be someday!"[58]

It is a particularly striking, even uncanny occurrence. Although Anne, the author as well as the character, did not know that the incident she described would have symbolic value, the reader must gasp, recognizing that this very ordinary anecdote points to the fate of the millions of Jews who were swept up in Nazi raids and burned in Nazi crematoria. In the destruction of the pen, Anne's own destruction is foreshadowed. The identity of pen and writer is strengthened by Anne's innocent concluding remark bestowing upon her fountain pen a wish of her own. The irony takes another twist, however, for although the tool for writing, the pen, was incinerated and the writer herself, Anne, was captured and died of typhus in a concentration camp, where many other Jews were incinerated, the diary itself, what was written, escaped destruction, although it was several times at risk itself, to stand as a witness. In a sense, the *Diary* and the story of Anne's life can be seen as symbolizing the struggle against meaninglessness and inhumanity, and thereby making that struggle the central theme of the diary.

In true literary fashion, however, the symbolism in Anne's *Diary* and her life is open to several possible interpretations, without invalidating this theme. A reader may see the *Diary* as suggesting that humans can overcome oppressive circumstances by exercising our common humanity even as it is being denied. Even when we are being victimized, we learn from Anne's *Diary*, we have the ability to resist victimization by bearing witness, no matter in what solitary fashion, to the terror confronting us. We resist by continuing to live, no matter in how contracted a manner, as human beings—learning, thinking, feeling, and growing, even if only for ourselves and inspired by an invisible hope.

The objection to this humanistic theme may be that it does not take into account the very real horrors we may suffer as human beings, which may rob us of all possibility of hope. This was, after all, Anne's fate and the fate of millions of others when Nazi viciousness barbarously exterminated them in ways beyond the power of language to condemn. Another theme, then, that we may draw from Anne's *Diary* and her life is not a hopeful one, but actually contradicts the hopeful theme suggested above. It is the bitter and despairing realization that despite our exercise of humanity, the force of inhumanity, of raw evil, may triumph and destroy us. And this seems, in many ways, unhappily, to be a greater truth.

But there is a third way of looking at Anne's *Diary* and

her life that seems to resolve the contradictions of these two opposing views. It is neither optimistic nor pessimistic, but spiritual, tragic, and redemptive (giving value to suffering). Anne believes in the redemptive aspect of the Jewish suffering:

> If we bear still this suffering and if there are still Jews left, when it is over, then Jews, instead of being doomed, will be held up as an example.[59]

In this view, Anne becomes a tragic sacrifice and a heroic figure because there is a force of some sort that hovers above the actions of men and women—God, the human spirit, history, fate—that allowed her *Diary* to survive although she did not. But in it and through it, she does survive as a voice for humanity, as an example of humanity, far more powerful than if she herself had remained alive. When she wrote, "If God lets me live ... I shall work in the world and for mankind!" she could not know that, by her death in the Holocaust and because of the way she lived her life, she would still work in the world and for mankind even if she did not live. She believed in God, humanity, and the future, despite the brutality of her times and despite her belief that there was something fundamentally destructive in people:

ON YOUR OWN
ACTIVITY #13

Choose three or four concrete events or situations Anne Frank recounts in her diary. Show how you can read them as being symbolic, as you can, for example, the incident of the loss of her fountain pen.

There's in people simply an urge to destroy, an urge to kill, to murder and rage, and until all mankind, without exception, undergoes a great change, wars will be waged, everything that has been built up, cultivated, and grown will be destroyed and disfigured, after which mankind will have to begin all over again.[60]

Toward the end of her diary, nevertheless, she wrote:

I still believe that people are really good at heart. I simply can't build up my hopes on a foundation consisting of confusion, misery, and death.[61]

Astoundingly, despite the weight of historical contradiction in the form of Nazi brutality, she was essentially right in her belief. For although humankind keeps repeating brutality and destructiveness, instances of moderation, goodness, humanity, and justice also recur. And Anne Frank, as she exists *through* her *Diary* is carrying out her ideals, not only by being an example of humanity in an inhuman era but by serving as an argument for goodness and humanity in every era.

7

The Aftermath

I twist my heart round ... so that the bad is on the outside and the good is on the inside and keep on trying to
find a way of becoming what I would so like to be, and
what I could be, if ... there weren't any other people living in the world.

THESE ARE THE LAST WORDS in her diary, "if ... there
weren't any other people living in the world." Anne wrote
them on August 1, 1944, three days before "other people," the
Gestapo (the Nazi secret police), broke in, arrested them, and

sent them all to horrible deaths, except Anne's father who managed to survive. It is an uncanny, eerie ending to the diary. Uncanny because of the foreboding in the words, but also because these words give a sense of formal completeness and closure to a work that is in reality unfinished.

The closing words of the *Diary* seem to signify, even without the terrible interruption, the end of the first stage of Anne's rite of passage from youth into adulthood. They mark the conclusion of an internal struggle we must all have with ourselves at those times when we grow into the next phase of our lives, when we enter the world and our meeting is not only with ourselves but with others. And the words Anne wrote on the inside back cover of her diary *"Soit gentil et tiens courage!"* ("Be good and have courage!") point in that direction.

Although the *Diary* is formally a complete work, an account of life in hiding and of a life in development, the story itself is incomplete. To know what happened, we must rely on sources other than Anne's *Diary*. We know what we do because the Nazis were meticulous keepers of records of their brutality and because of the testimony of survivors.

ON YOUR OWN
ACTIVITY #14

After researching the subject, write an essay on what the Allied forces (the soldiers of the United States, the Soviet Union, and England) found when they liberated Nazi concentration camps at the end of the war.

WHAT HAPPENED TO THE PEOPLE TAKEN FROM THE SECRET ANNEX?

When the eight Jews were arrested on the morning of August 4, 1944, two of their helpers, Victor Kugler and Johannes Kleiman, were also arrested. Two others, Miep Gies and Elisabeth Voskuijl, were not. It was Miep Gies who found and preserved Anne's diary and gave it to Otto Frank after the war.

Mr. Kugler and Mr. Kleiman were taken to prison in Amsterdam and scheduled to be sent to a German labor camp. Mr. Kleiman suffered a gastric hemorrhage and was released in September, unfit for any kind of labor. Prison records show he was sent home. He soon returned to Opekta, now called Gies & Co., as its manager, and died in 1959. Mr. Kugler managed to escape in March 1945 while on a forced march into Germany when the German troops leading the march were attacked by British planes. He hid with farmers and managed to bicycle back to

ON YOUR OWN
ACTIVITY #15

On the Internet, visit the Yad Vashem website. Yad Vashem is a museum in Jerusalem established as a memorial to the millions of Jews murdered by the Nazis. It contains the world's largest repository of information on the Holocaust, and it is dedicated to education, commemoration, research and documentation regarding the Holocaust, or Shoah, as it is called in Hebrew. *www.yadvashem.org/* is its web address. After you have visited the site, write a letter to a friend describing what you learned from the site and the thoughts and feelings with which the experience left you.

Amsterdam. In 1955, he emigrated to Canada, where he died in 1989.

The eight Jews were taken from a prison in Amsterdam to Westerbork, a transit camp for Jews in the north of Holland. From there, they were to be transported to extermination camps in Poland. They were kept in Westerbork throughout August 1944. We know something of Anne's life in Westerbork because of the testimony of Mrs. de Wiek, who was in Westerbork when the Franks and their friends arrived, and who survived:

> I saw Anne Frank and Peter van Daan every day in Westerbork. They were always together, and I often said to my husband: "Look at those two beautiful young people...."
>
> In Westerbork Anne was lovely, so radiant that her beauty flowed over into Peter. She was very pallid at first, but there was something so intensely attractive about her frailty and her expressive face....
>
> Perhaps it's not the right expression to say that Anne's eyes were radiant. But they had a glow.... And her movements, her looks, had such a lilt to them that I often asked myself: Can she possibly be happy?
>
> She was happy in Westerbork, though that seems almost incredible, for things were hard for us in the camp....
>
> You ask me what Anne's mother was like? There in Westerbork she was quiet; she seemed numbed all the time, and I did not know her before the camp. She no longer talked very much. Margot, too, spoke little, but Edith Frank could have been a mute. She said nothing at work, and in the evenings she was always washing underclothing. The water was murky and there was no soap, but she went on washing, all the time.
>
> Anne's father was quiet, too, but it was a reassuring quietness that helped Anne and helped the rest of us, too. He lived

in the men's barracks, but once when Anne was sick he came over to visit her every evening and would stand beside her bed for hours, telling her stories. Anne was so like him that when she recovered and David fell ill, a twelve-year-old boy who lived in the women's barracks with us, she acted in just the same way, stood by his bed and talked to him. David came from an orthodox family, and he and Anne always talked about God.... That was in Westerbork. Anne was happy there, although we weren't yet in safety nor at the end of our misery.[62]

The Franks, the van Pels (whom Anne called van Daan) and Mr. Pfeffer, the dentist (whom Anne called Dussel), were transported along with 1,011 others on September 3, 1944, to the Auschwitz concentration camp. Mr. van Pels, along with 549 of these people, including all children under 15, was gassed to death there on September 6. Otto saw him marched to the gas chamber. According to records recovered at Auschwitz, Mr. Pfeffer was sent to the Neuengamme camp and killed there. According to a Netherlands Red Cross file, Edith Frank died in the Auschwitz-Birkenau camp on January 6, 1945. Mrs. van Pels, Peter's mother, was sent from one Nazi camp to another, from Auschwitz to Belsen, from there to Buchenwald, and then to Theresienstadt. The Dutch Red Cross reported that she died "between April 9 and May 8, 1945, in Germany or in Czechoslovakia."[63] Peter died on a forced march out of Auschwitz some time in January 1945. Otto "was in the infirmary [at Auschwitz] at the time, and he had tried to persuade Peter to hide [there] also, but Peter did not dare," according to Mrs. De Wiek.[64]

Margot and Anne were taken to Bergen-Belsen, a camp filthy with lice and a plague of typhus. The prisoners lived in tents and slept on straw on the ground. The weather was foul and the wind blew harshly. Photographs taken when British troops arrived after the war show piles of boney skeletons tossed upon each other. It was there that Margot and then Anne died of typhus in March 1945, just weeks before the camp's liberation by British troops.

In Bergen-Belsen, Anne met her school friend Lies, who had been deported from Amsterdam in 1943. When Lies saw the new prisoners in 1945 arrive at a block of the camp next to where she was imprisoned,

> I stole out of the barrack, went over to the barbed wire, and called softly into the darkness: "Is anyone over there?"
>
> A voice answered: "I am here. I am Mrs. van Daan." We had known the van Daans in Amsterdam. I told her who I was, and asked whether Margot or Anne could come to the fence. Mrs. van Daan answered in a breathless voice that Margot was ill, but that Anne could probably come, and she would go to look for her.
>
> I waited, shivering in the darkness. It took a long time. But suddenly I heard a voice: "Lies, Lies? Where are you?" It was Anne, and I ran in the direction of the voice, and then I saw her beyond the barbed wire. She was in rags. I saw her emaciated, sunken face in the darkness. Her eyes were very large. We cried and cried, for now there was only the barbed wire between us, nothing more. And no longer any difference in our fates.
>
> I told Anne that my mother had died and my father was dying, and Anne told me that she knew nothing about her father, but that her mother had stayed behind in Auschwitz. Only Margot was still with her, but she was already very ill. They had met Mrs. van Daan again only after their arrival here in Belsen.

But there was a difference between us, after all. I was in a block where we still occasionally had parcels. Anne had nothing at all. She was freezing, and starving. I called to her in a whisper:

"I'll see what I can do, Anne. Maybe ... come back here tomorrow, will you?"

And Anne called across: "Yes, tomorrow. I'll come."

I saw Anne again, for she came to the fence on the following night. I had packed up a woolen jacket and some biscuits and sugar and a tin of sardines for her. I called out: "Anne, watch now!" Then I threw the bundle across. But I heard only screams and Anne crying, and I shouted: "Anne, what's happened?" And she called back, weeping: "A woman caught it and won't give it to me." Then I heard rapid footsteps as the woman ran away. I said: "Anne, come again. I'll see what else I can find...." Next time I had only a pair of stockings and biscuits, but this time she caught it.[65]

And that is the last report that we have of Anne Frank alive.

THE DIARY OF ANNE FRANK

Otto Frank was liberated from Auschwitz on January 27, 1945, by the Russian armies that were advancing toward Berlin. His trip back to the Netherlands took him through Odessa (in the south of the Soviet Union) and through Marseilles, France. During the trip, he met Elfriede Geringer-Markovits, who had been a neighbor of the Franks in Amsterdam and was deported to Auschwitz with her entire family on May 19, 1944. Her husband and son perished, and she returned only with her daughter, who had known Anne. "[A]t one of the stops made by the train taking them away from Auschwitz, [she told] her,

'I've just seen Anne Frank's father.'"[66] Otto and Elfriede married in November 1953 and lived in Basel, Switzerland, where Otto died in 1980.

When Otto returned to Amsterdam, he reestablished contact with Miep Gies and her husband, Jan, and lived with them for seven years. On the day that he learned that Anne was dead, Miep Gies gave him her diary, which she had been keeping to give back to Anne when she returned.

During the time in the Secret Annex, Anne had decided, after hearing a Dutch Member of Parliament in a broadcast from London say that "they ought to make a collection of diaries and letters after the war," that she was going to turn hers into a novel.[67] Anne began rewriting the diary with the hope of publishing it someday.

Soon after the war, Otto read sections of the diary to his friend Dr. Werner Cahn, who had friends in the Dutch publishing world. Cahn showed it to a well-known Dutch historian, Dr. Jan Romein, who read it in one night and wrote an awestruck article about Anne and her diary, which was published on April 3, 1946, in the Dutch journal *Het Parool* (*The Word*).[68] Because of this article, Anne's diary was published as *Het Achtrehuis* (*The House in the Rear*) in 1947 in the Netherlands and was immensely successful. German and French translations were published in 1950, and the English translation of the diary was published in England and the United States in 1952 and again was acclaimed not only as a significant historical document of the Holocaust but as an astonishing work of literature. It has been translated into nearly 60 languages and more than 16 million copies of the *Diary* have been sold. The *Diary* became the basis of an award-winning Broadway play and a Hollywood movie, and Anne Frank became a legendary figure.

The authenticity of the *Diary*, however, was challenged, usually by people like the French academic Robert Faurisson, who has made a career out of denying that the Holocaust actually happened and that Nazi gas chambers even existed. In response to these challenges, the Netherlands State Institute for War Documentation and the Dutch State Forensic Science Laboratory subjected the original manuscripts of the diary to a careful examination, which included handwriting analysis, and concluded that Anne Frank's *Diary* is indeed authentic.

1. There are three editions of Anne Frank's *Diary* published in English. The original English edition of 1952, based on the Dutch edition of 1947, was established by her father Otto Frank and is called *The Diary of a Young Girl*. It is this edition in its many translations that has become a worldwide classic and best-seller. In 1989, the English translation of the 1986 Dutch edition called *The Diary of Anne Frank: The Critical Edition* was published. This edition contains the original edition of Anne's diary and all of Anne's original diary manuscripts, her first draft, and the revisions of the draft that she began. It also contains documentary material attesting to the authenticity of the diary as well as historical essays concerning the diary. In 1991, a new English edition, edited by Otto Frank and Mirjam Pressler, incorporating material collated from Anne's original and revised manuscripts was published as *Anne Frank: The Diary of a Young Girl: The Definitive Edition*. Citation in this essay will usually be from the 1952 edition. When citation is from other editions, that will be indicated and, when possible, parallel reference to the 1952 edition will be given.

2. Anne Frank. *The Diary of a Young Girl*. Translated from the Dutch by B.M. Mooyaart-Doubleday. New York: The Modern Library, 1952, p. 16–18.

3. Otto Frank and Mirjam Pressler, ed. *The Diary of a Young Girl: The Definitive Edition*. Translated from the Dutch by Susan Massotty. New York: Doubleday, 1991, p. 2. Anne Frank, *The Diary of a Young Girl*, p. 12.

4. Anne Frank, *The Diary of a Young Girl*, p. 11.

5. "The Story of Miep Gies." Scholastic.com Website: *http://teacher.scholastic.com /frank/miep.htm*.

6. David Barnouw and Gerold Van Der Stroom, ed. *The Diary of Anne Frank: The Critical Edition*. Prepared by the Netherlands State Institute for War Documentation, translated from the Dutch by Arnold J. Ponerans and B.M. Mooyaart-Doubleday. New York: Doubleday, 1989, p. 177.

7. Otto Frank and Mirjam Pressler, *The Diary of a Young Girl: The Definitive Edition*, p. 1.

8. Anne Frank, *The Diary of a Young Girl*, p. 13.

9. Ibid.

10. Anne Frank, *The Diary of a Young Girl*, p. 15.

11. Anne Frank, *The Diary of a Young Girl*, p. 24.

12. Otto Frank and Mirjam Pressler, *The Diary of a Young Girl: The Definitive Edition*, p. 252ff. Anne

Frank, *The Diary of a Young Girl*, p. 213–215.

13. Anne Frank, *The Diary of a Young Girl*, p. 78.

14. Otto Frank and Mirjam Pressler, *The Diary of a Young Girl: The Definitive Edition*, p. 60–61.

15. Otto Frank and Mirjam Pressler, *The Diary of a Young Girl: The Definitive Edition*, p. 276. Anne Frank, *The Diary of a Young Girl*, pp. 232–233.

16. Otto Frank and Mirjam Pressler, *The Diary of a Young Girl: The Definitive Edition*, pp. 6–7. Anne Frank, *The Diary of a Young Girl*, p. 12–13.

17. Otto Frank and Mirjam Pressler, *The Diary of a Young Girl: The Definitive Edition*, p. 18. Anne Frank, *The Diary of a Young Girl*, p. 22.

18. Otto Frank and Mirjam Pressler, *The Diary of a Young Girl: The Definitive Edition*, p. 22. Anne Frank, *The Diary of a Young Girl*, p. 26.

19. Otto Frank and Mirjam Pressler, *The Diary of a Young Girl: The Definitive Edition*, pp. 79–80. Anne Frank, *The Diary of a Young Girl*, p. 74–75.

20. Otto Frank and Mirjam Pressler, *The Diary of a Young Girl: The Definitive Edition*, p. 80.

21. Otto Frank and Mirjam Pressler, *The Diary of a*

Young Girl: The Definitive Edition, p. 81.

22. Anne Frank, *The Diary of a Young Girl*, p. 154.

23. Anne Frank, *The Diary of a Young Girl*, p. 143.

24. Anne Frank, *The Diary of a Young Girl*, p. 143–144.

25. Anne Frank, *The Diary of a Young Girl*, p. 144.

26. Ibid.

27. Anne Frank, *The Diary of a Young Girl*, p. 155.

28. Anne Frank, *The Diary of a Young Girl*, p. 155–156.

29. Anne Frank, *The Diary of a Young Girl*, p. 169.

30. Ibid.

31. Anne Frank, *The Diary of a Young Girl*, p. 166.

32. Ibid.

33. Anne Frank, *The Diary of a Young Girl*, p. 170–171.

34. Anne Frank, *The Diary of a Young Girl*, p. 171.

35. Anne Frank, *The Diary of a Young Girl*, p. 264.

36. Anne Frank, *The Diary of a Young Girl*, p. 277.

37. Anne Frank, *The Diary of a Young Girl*, p. 260.

38. Anne Frank, *The Diary of a Young Girl*, p. 280–283.

39. Anne Frank, *The Diary of a Young Girl*, p. 274–275.

40. Anne Frank, *The Diary of a Young Girl*, p. 65.

41. Anne Frank, *The Diary of a Young Girl*, p. 271.

42. Otto Frank and Mirjam Pressler, *The Diary of a Young Girl: The Definitive Edition*, p. 63. Anne Frank, *The Diary of a Young Girl*, p. 56.

43. Anne Frank, *The Diary of a Young Girl*, p. 150.

44. Anne Frank, *The Diary of a Young Girl*, p. 184.

45. Anne Frank, *The Diary of a Young Girl*, p. 267–268.

46. Otto Frank and Mirjam Pressler, *The Diary of a Young Girl: The Definitive Edition*, p. 226 Anne Frank, *The Diary of a Young Girl*, p. 194.

47. Otto Frank and Mirjam Pressler, *The Diary of a Young Girl: The Definitive Edition*, p. 226. Anne Frank, *The Diary of a Young Girl*, p. 194.

48. Anne Frank, *The Diary of a Young Girl*, p. 266.

49. Otto Frank and Mirjam Pressler, *The Diary of a Young Girl: The Definitive Edition*, p. 101.

50. Anne Frank, *The Diary of a Young Girl*, p. 98–100.

51. Anne Frank, *The Diary of a Young Girl*, p. 150.

52. Anne Frank, *The Diary of a Young Girl*, p. 196.

53. Anne Frank, *The Diary of a Young Girl*, p. 189.

54. "The Story of Miep Gies." Scholastic.com Website: *http://teacher.scholastic.com /frank/miep.htm.*

55. Anne Frank, *The Diary of a Young Girl*, p. 33.

56. Otto Frank and Mirjam Pressler, *The Diary of a Young Girl: The Definitive Edition*, p. 142. Anne Frank, *The Diary of a Young Girl*, p. 126.

57. Anne Frank, *The Diary of a Young Girl*, p. 128.

58. Otto Frank and Mirjam Pressler, *The Diary of a Young Girl: The Definitive Edition*, pp. 146–147. Anne Frank, *The Diary of a Young Girl*, p. 128–130.

59. Anne Frank, *The Diary of a Young Girl*, p. 221.

60. Anne Frank, *The Diary of a Young Girl*, p. 237.

61. Anne Frank, *The Diary of a Young Girl*, p. 279.

62. Ernst Schnabel. *The Footsteps of Anne Frank.* Translated from the German by Richard and Clara Winston. London: Longmans, Green, 1959, p. 125–127.

63. David Barnouw and Gerold Van Der Stroom, *The Diary of Anne Frank: The Critical Edition*, p. 52.

64. Ernst Schnabel, *The Footsteps of Anne Frank*, p. 139.

65. Ernst Schnabel, *The Footsteps of Anne Frank*, pp. 144–145, 153–154.

66. David Barnouw and Gerold Van Der Stroom, *The Diary of Anne Frank: The Critical Edition*, p. 55.

67. Anne Frank, *The Diary of a Young Girl*, p. 205.

68. David Barnouw and Gerold Van Der Stroom, *The Diary of Anne Frank: The Critical Edition*, p. 67.

Barnouw, David, and Gerold Van Der Stroom, ed. *The Diary of Anne Frank: The Critical Edition*. Prepared by the Netherlands State Institute for War Documentation, translated from the Dutch by Arnold J. Ponerans and B.M. Mooyaart-Doubleday. New York: Doubleday, 1989.

Frank, Anne. *The Diary of a Young Girl*. Translated from the Dutch by B.M. Mooyaart-Doubleday. New York: The Modern Library, 1952.

Frank, Otto, and Mirjam Pressler, ed. *The Diary of a Young Girl: The Definitive Edition*. Translated from the Dutch by Susan Massotty. New York: Doubleday, 1991.

Schnabel, Ernst. *The Footsteps of Anne Frank*. Translated from the German by Richard and Clara Winston. London: Longmans, Green, 1959.

"The Story of Miep Gies." Scholastic.com Website: *http://teacher.scholastic.com/frank/miep.htm.*

Brenner, Rachel Feldhay. *Writing as Resistance: Four Women Confronting the Holocaust, Edith Stein, Simone Weil, Anne Frank, Etty Hillesum.* University Park, PA: Pennsylvania State University Press, 1997.

Enzer, Hyman Aaron and Sandra Solotaroff-Enzer, eds. *Anne Frank: Reflections on Her Life and Legacy.* Urbana, IL: University of Illinois Press, 2000.

Geis, Miep and Alison Leslie Gold. *Anne Frank Remembered: The Story of the Woman Who Helped to Hide the Frank Family.* New York, NY: Simon, 1987.

Lee, Carol Anne. *Roses from the Earth: The Biography of Anne Frank.* London, UK: Viking, 1999.

Levin, Meyer. *The Obsession.* New York, NY: Simon and Schuster, 1973.

Melnick, Ralph. *The Stolen Legacy of Anne Frank: Meyer Levin, Lillian Hellman, and the Staging of the Diary.* New Haven, CT: Yale University Press, 1997.

Muller, Melissa. *Anne Frank.* Translated by Rita and Robert Kimber. New York, NY: Metropolitan Books, 1998.

Novick, Peter. *The Holocaust in American Life.* Boston, MA: Houghton Mifflin, 1999.

Ozick, Cynthia. "Who Owns Anne Frank?" *New Yorker* (October 6, 1997): 76–87.

Ravits, Martha. "Anne Frank (1929-1945)" *http://www.routledge-ny.com/ ref/ holocaustlit/annefrank.pdf*

———. "To Work in the World: Anne Frank and American Literary History." *Women's Studies: An Interdisciplinary Journal* 27 (1997): 1–30.

Rittner, Carol, ed. *Anne Frank in the World: Essays and Reflections.* Armond, NY: Sharpe, 1998.

Thurman, Judith. "Not Even a Nice Girl." *New Yorker* (December 18, 1989): 166–120.

Waaldijk, Berteke. "Reading Anne Frank as a Woman." *Women's Studies International Forum* 16 (1993): 327–335.

Websites

The Anne Frank Center

www.annefrank.com

Anne Frank Museum Amsterdam

www.annefrank.org

Anne Frank the Writer: An Unfinished Story

www.ushmm.org/museum/exhibit/online/af/htmlsite/

page:

A-1: © Anne Frank-Fonds, Basel

A-2: © Anne Frank-Fonds, Basel

B: © Anne Frank-Fonds, Basel

C: © Anne Frank-Fonds, Basel

D-1: ©2003 Getty Images

D-2: © Anne Frank-Fonds, Basel

E-1: © Getty Images|Hulton Archives

E-2: Getty Images|Hulton Archives

F: © Anne Frank-Fonds, Basel

G: © Anne Frank-Fonds, Basel

H: © Anne Frank-Fonds, Basel

I: © Anne Frank-Fonds, Basel

J: Yivo Institute for Jewish Research

Cover: © Handout/Reuters/CORBIS

ACKNOWLEDGMENTS

Ernst Schnabel, *Anne Frank Spur eines Kindes: Ein Bericht.* © Fischer Taschenbuch Verlag Gmbtt, Frankfurt am Main, 1997.

From *Anne Frank: The Diary of a Young Girl* by Anne Frank, translated by B.M. Mooyaart-Doubleday, © 1952 by Otto H. Frank. Used by permission of Doubleday, a division of Random House, Inc.

From *The Diary of Anne Frank: The Critical Edition* by Anne Frank, © 1986 by Anne Frank-Fonds, Basle/Switzerland, for all texts of Anne Frank. English Translation copyright © 1989 by Doubleday, a division of Random House Inc., and by Penguin Books Ltd. Used by permission of Doubleday, a division of Random House Inc.

From *The Diary of a Young Girl: The Definitive Edition* by Anne Frank. Otto H. Frank & Mirjam Pressler, Editors, translated by Susan Massotty, © 1995 by Doubleday, a division of Random House Inc. Used by permission of Doubleday, a division of Random House Inc.

NEIL HEIMS is a freelance writer, editor, and researcher. He has a Ph.D. in English from the City University of New York. He has written on a number of authors including Albert Camus, Arthur Miller, John Milton, and J.R.R. Tolkien.